# DIY CRAFTS & PROJECTS

## FOR YOUR

## INSTANT POT

# DIY CRAFTS & PROJECTS

## FOR YOUR

## INSTANT POT

Lip Balm, Tie-Dye, Candles,
and Dozens of Other Amazing Ideas!

### DAVID MURPHY

Racehorse Publishing

Racehorse Publishing books may be purchased in bulk at special discounts for sales promotion, corporate gifts, fund-raising, or educational purposes. Special editions can also be created to specifications. For details, contact the Special Sales Department, Skyhorse Publishing, 307 West 36th Street, 11th Floor, New York, NY 10018 or info@skyhorsepublishing.com.

Racehorse Publishing™ is a pending trademark of Skyhorse Publishing, Inc.®, a Delaware corporation.

Visit our website at www.skyhorsepublishing.com.

10 9 8 7 6 5 4 3 2 1

Library of Congress Cataloging-in-Publication Data

Names: Murphy, David (Cook), author.
Title: Instant Pot crafts and projects: lip balm, tie dye, candles, and dozens of other amazing pressure cooker ideas / David Murphy.
Description: New York, NY: Racehorse Publishing, [2019] | Includes bibliographical references and index.
Identifiers: LCCN 2019011275 (print) | LCCN 2019014025 (ebook) | ISBN 9781510746176 (Ebook) | ISBN 9781510746169 (alk. paper)
Subjects: LCSH: Wax craft. | Ointments. | Food craft. | Soap. | Smart cookers.
Classification: LCC TT866 (ebook) | LCC TT866 .M87 2019 (print) | DDC 731/.2—dc23
LC record available at https://lccn.loc.gov/2019011275

Cover design by Peter Donahue
Cover photos by David Murphy

Print ISBN: 978-1-5107-4616-9
Ebook ISBN: 978-1-5107-4617-6

Printed in China

*I would like to give a special thanks to my Stephen, and his constant patience, side comments, and eye rolls for every time I said, "I have to go to the store again." I love you always.*

*Thank you to all of my family members and friends that continue to support me, give me constant love, and push me to always think differently than others.*

# Contents

# Introduction

- - - - - - - - - - - - - - - - - - - -

Thank you so much for purchasing this book! I have been dying to create a book like this for a while, and I'm so ecstatic to get it out there to everyone. If you haven't had a chance to purchase my other book, *Instant Pot Magic: 50 Surprising Recipes for Beer, Jam, Bread, and More!*, then you're totally missing out on some amazing tips and recipes! That's the cookbook that is leading the revolution of being able to think differently about the Instant Pot, and how to do more than just dump ingredients in and expect it to cook an amazing meal. There are plenty of fabulous recipes like that, but I like pushing things a bit further.

There is an overall message between my first book and this book. That message? Don't be afraid to use your Instant Pot, and learn to incorporate the Instant Pot into your daily life, just like you would a favorite kitchen spoon.

Think about it for a moment—every time we cook something, we reach for our wooden spoon to start stirring the food in pot, pan, or a pitcher to mix a beverage.

I want people to use the Instant Pot in the same exact manner.

Do you need to sauté some vegetables? Use your Instant Pot!

Do you want to make a quick chicken noodle soup? Use your Instant Pot!

Want to make the most tender pieces of meat you'll ever eat? Use your Instant Pot!

Let the Instant Pot become your best friend, and it will never let you down.

In the effort to continually push myself to think and do differently, I've assembled this book full of the most creative things that I have been able to make in the Instant Pot.

You're not going to have pull out any pots or pans to use your Instant Pot to make any of the hacks, crafts, or home and beauty items. If you're a DIY'er and Instant Pot fanatic like I am, then you're going to fall in love with everything in here! There's even some kid-friendly projects that would be fun to work on with your children.

If you get anything out of my book, I hope you get this: to embrace your Instant Pot, and not be afraid to create with it!

With all of that said, there are a couple of things that I would like to mention.

One, there's a couple of recipes that call for you to use alcohol. Please note that Instant Pot does not condone using alcohol in your Instant Pot. The biggest concern is alcohol vapors that can be released in the "cooking" process. So, please do not have your Instant Pot by any type of open flame as a precaution, and be sure that you have a well-ventilated area.

Two, I am using the Instant Pot DUO Plus 60, 6 quart 9-in-1 model. I love this model so much that I actually have two of them! This model has a Yogurt function button on it, and that allows it to do less heat. Being able to increase and lessen the heat function and pressure function settings on this Instant Pot is why it's my absolute favorite model.

I truly hope you enjoy this book and that it inspires you to create!

# Some Instant Pot Terminology

In this book, I'm going to be using a lot of abbreviations and terminology that I want you to get used to seeing all over the place, especially in online recipes and the Instant Pot Facebook community.

**5-5-5:** This is a common cooking method that all Pot Heads love to use for making hard-boiled eggs: 5 minutes HMP, 5 minutes NPR, and 5 minutes in an ice bath.

**Double-Boil Method:** You're used to doing this on the stove top. Well, now we're doing it in our Instant Pots! To help ensure that your bowls or containers don't get stuck into your IP, use a thick piece of foil crimped onto the rim that the bowl is laying on, or use a big binder clip to attach to the rim of your IP.

The first way uses a binder clip. We want to make sure that the top bowl we are preparing items in doesn't sit flat into the Instant Pot, or you run the chance of having your bowl and the Instant Pot liner getting stuck together. If that happens, it's not fun to try to pull the two apart.

The other way is to take a piece of foil, and fold it over into a thick fold to act as a wedge on the rim of the Instant Pot for the bowl to rest on while allowing some steam to release.

**HMP:** High Manual Pressure.

**Inner Pot:** This is the metal pot that goes inside the machine. A lot of people call it the inner pot or pot liner.

**IP:** Instant Pot—not Insta Pot. Just to help clear up any confusion!

**LMP:** Low Manual Pressure.

**NPR or NR:** Natural Pressure Release. The Instant Pot has a pressure-release valve at the top of the lid. NPR means that you will NOT open the pressure-release vent. You will let the pot depressurize naturally. This process can take anywhere between 20–35 minutes, dependent on your recipe and your elevation.

**PIP:** Pot in Pot. This is a common cooking process to use with your instant pot. It means that you have ingredients that you're cooking in one pot, which then is placed on a trivet in your Instant Pot. I do a lot of PIP cooking in this book, and you'll see how easy it is.

**Pot Head:** An Instant Pot user!

**QPR or QR:** Quick Pressure Release. This means to open the pressure-release valve on top of your Instant Pot lid. It will only take a couple of minutes to depressurize. Once your pressure pin drops, you're safe to open your lid.

**Sling:** This is the process of taking a piece of foil and flattening it out into about a 2-inch width. You place this under the container or food that you are cooking in your Instant Pot. This aids in the removal of food from your IP. The IP can get really hot, and foil cools faster, so it is easier to touch and remove.

# How to Clean Your Instant Pot

*Before cleaning your machine, it is best to make sure that it is unplugged from any electrical outlet. These are tips that I have found work best to keep my Instant Pot maintained and working like a well-oiled machine.*

1. Remove the inner silicone ring from the lid. This easily pulls off, and easily goes back on. The first time I did this I thought I was going to break my lid. Don't worry—it'll be fine! You can wash this with this warm soapy water, or wash in the top rack of your dishwasher.

2. Remove the metal basket covering the vent knob steam release valve. Wash the metal basket with warm soapy water.

3. Remove the silicone tip from the float valve. Just be sure your fingers are on the opposite side to catch the pressure pin. You don't want to lose it and have to order another one. You can wash this with warm soapy water.

4. Remove the pressure pin. You will see the upper part where the steam is released from is dirty. Warm soapy water will clean this perfectly.

**5.** Clean the pressure pin hole. The external top area of the pressure pin area can get really dirty because of the venting and pressurizing process. Particles from ingredients can get lodged in there. Clean with warm soapy water and a small bristle brush.

**6.** Remove the condensation cup on the side of the machine. If you don't keep this area regularly maintained, mold and mildew can grow. That's something you never want to happen to your beloved machine! After each use, I always wash with warm soapy water to keep it clean.

**7.** With wet Q-tips, clean inside the rim of the machine. Food particles can get stuck to the lid, and I've found this method of cleaning underneath the lip of the machine is easier. Sometimes I will take a folded piece of paper towel to clean under them as well.

**8.** Inside the machine itself can get dirty from ingredients, especially if you have a little overflow that might have occurred from making your favorite pot of chili or soup. Take a slightly damp wash-cloth, and wipe around the inside of the machine. You don't want it saturated with water, just wet enough to clean up any debris that might be inside the well of your machine.

9. The Instant Pot's metal liner can get seriously dirty from constant use. Many people use the product Bar Keeper's Friend; however, I love using baking soda. If you use 2 tablespoons of baking soda, ¼ cup of warm water, and a green scrubbing pad, you will have an amazingly clean metal pot! Your metal liner is completely dishwasher safe, so don't be afraid to put it into your machine. I only offer this way of cleaning it if your pot becomes a little stained with dried-on foods, if you burned food on it, if grains of rice left impressions, or if you have any type of discoloration. Because the Instant Pot metal liner is made of stainless steel, a rainbow effect can happen. It just comes from cooking on high heat and is a natural effect that happens to most stainless steel cooking products. Using baking soda, water, and a green scrubby pad seems to get rid of the rainbow effect as well.

This section is so close to my heart. There is nothing better than a great-smelling home, and I love being able to pinch a penny here and there. Thanks to having a family of five (and two dogs), I'm always trying to find ways to economize—yes, I'm a total couponer. By being able to make my own wax melts (a small obsession of mine!), detergent, and saline solution, I'm able to save a few extra dollars in the end.

A lot of these ideas I'm sharing with you are versatile, so you can mix up the scents by using different essential oils, change the color of the scented wax melts or candles with candle dye (or even shavings from other candles!), and so much more. The only thing that'll stop you is your own imagination.

This section is just a gateway to what you can use your Instant Pot for. Yes, I know. Pulling out your Instant Pot to make a candle or soak wood chips is not the first thing that comes to mind; however, I'm here to try to help change your way of thinking in a fun, new, and inventive way!

# Household
# Tricks

# CONCENTRATED LIQUID LAUNDRY DETERGENT

**Makes approximately 1½ gallons concentrated detergent, which will make about 18 gallons of detergent**

*When you have a family as big as I do, then you're always look for budget-friendly ways to cook and clean. This recipe has been around for years, and I translated it to be used in the Instant Pot. By the time you're done making this, you'll wind up with a product that truly resembles detergent. You'll have super clean clothes that smell amazingly fresh. You can easily find these products at your local grocery or online.*

## Directions

1. Add all ingredients into your pot. Press Sauté button.

2. Allow mixture to get really hot until it almost starts to boil.

3. Press the Cancel button, and then press the Yogurt button.

4. "Cook" your detergent on the yogurt function for approximately 20–25 minutes, or until all of the grated soap is dissolved.

5. Once done, turn pot off by hitting the Cancel button. Pour mixture into a pitcher or another container and allow 24 hours to cool.

6. You will get a slime-like consistency once cool.

7. Use 1 cup of this detergent and mix with 7–7½ cups of water. Mix well. Reuse your detergent bottles to make life easy!

## Ingredients

½ bar Fels-Naptha soap (grated)
⅓ cup borax
⅓ cup Arm & Hammer Super Washing Soda
1 gallon water

# SCENTED WAX MELTS

**Makes 3–6 packs of wax melts**

*Do you love using your favorite scented wax melts, but hate having to buy so many and spend so much money? Then I must be speaking your language with this easy DIY project. If you don't want to spend money on wax dyes, then don't worry about adding color to them. However, if you do want to add color to your wax melts, then simply save wax from your old candles that you're about to throw away.*

## Directions

1. In a bowl (using double-boil method on page xi), add all ingredients. Stir occasionally until thoroughly melted.

2. Remove bowl from pot, and pour wax mixture into molds.

3. Allow to cool before using. You can place in freezer to harden faster.

4. You can add any of your favorite essential oils or use whatever wax dyes you wish to.

## Ingredients

6 Tbsp. white beeswax
½ cup + 2 Tbsp. coconut oil
15 drops cucumber essential oil
10 drops lime essential oil
1 tsp. light green wax dye
Wax molds (you can easily get these from any online retailer, reuse your old ones, or go to a craft store)

# RECYCLED CANDLE JARS

*Since I have a newfound love for making my own candles in my Instant Pot, I've found it to be very easy to simply clean old candleholders I have to repurpose. I love being able to upcycle and reuse products like this! With this quick candle-cleaning hack, you'll be taking jars from your friends' homes (ask first!) to repurpose them for your own new candles you get to make!*

## Directions

1. Cover the top of each jar with a piece of foil.

2. Put 4 cups of warm water into your Instant Pot liner, and place trivet into the bottom. Press the Steam button and adjust time to 5 minutes. You're not going to need it on that long.

3. Once you see steam starting to rise, place your foil-topped candle jars onto the trivet and place the lid on top.

4. Wait approximately 3 minutes, and carefully remove each jar with oven-safe mitts. These jars will be hot. Carefully remove the foil from the tops and then pour the wax onto the paper plate. Moisten the paper towels with a little bit of hot water to wipe away any leftover wax and dirt from inside the lip of the candle. Repeat the process for each candle that you're cleaning.

## Ingredients

Old candle jars

Aluminum foil

4 cups warm water

Trivet

A lid for your Instant Pot, not the pressure cooker lid

Paper plate

Paper towels

# HOMEMADE CANDLES

**Makes 5 (5-oz.) jars**

*Let's face it—buying candles can turn into an expensive habit very quickly. Sure, you can get cheaper ones, but that scent and quality aren't always there. Making candles is not as difficult to do as you might think, especially with your handy Instant Pot readily available at your side! You will now have the flexibility to create whatever color and scented candles you want. In fact, you can even repurpose candles into different candleholders! It's what I did with this project. I recycled some red apple/cinnamon scented candles that were almost done, and I converted them into something new.*

## Directions

1. Set up your Instant Pot in a double-boil method (page xi). Place 4 cups of warm water into your IP, and put wax into the bowl that you're placing on top to melt. Press the Steam button, and set the time for approximately 25 minutes. Stir wax occasionally to help the melting process.

2. While waiting for wax to melt, crimp together wick tabs and ropes for as many candles as you want to make.

3. Once your wax has melted, you can add in your fragrance oils and stir well. You can also add in any type of wax coloring that you wish to, as well. Remove your bowl of wax from the heat source, and allow to cool for 3–4 minutes.

4. After your 3–4 minutes have passed, pour wax into your candle jars. Once you see the wax starting to solidify around the base of your candleholder, you can insert your candle wick. You can use a straw or a long thin stick to push into the bottom of your jar. Lay the pencil across the jar, and allow the wick to rest on top of it. This will ensure that your wick doesn't get formed and folded into your candle.

5. Once completely cooled, you can start enjoying your candle!

## Ingredients

4 cups warm water
Unscented soy wax
Candle wick tabs
Candle wick rope
Fragrance oils
Heatproof candle containers
    (I love reusing my old candle jars
    for this project—see page 7!)
Pencil

# SINUS SALINE SOLUTION

**Makes 2 cups**

*I suffer from chronic allergies, and have been using saline solution rinses since I was a teenager. It's been one of the most amazing things that my sinus specialist taught me how to do. Now when I get allergy attacks throughout the year or a sinus infection, I reach for my own saline solution and start irrigating. This simple solution is so easy to make in a breeze for whenever your sinus needs a little irrigation. Please note that it takes about 7–8 minutes of boiling for the pin to pop-up, and the CDC states that water must be boiled for at least 3–5 minutes to kill micro-organisms. Also, please allow your saline solution to come to room temperature before using, and don't keep the leftovers.*

## Directions

1. Add all ingredients into your pot and stir.
2. Press Sauté button, close and lock lid, and close the vent.
3. Once the pressure pin has popped up, press the Cancel button. QPR any pressure.
4. Remove lid and pour solution into a clean container. Allow to cool completely before using to irrigate sinuses.

## Ingredients

2 cups water
1 tsp. sea salt
1 tsp. baking soda

# SUPER-SIMPLE AIR FRESHENER

**Air freshener will last all day!**

*Do you want to make your whole home smell amazing, but don't want to burn a lot of candles to achieve this goal? Pour some potpourri into your Instant Pot, add warm water, and you have your very own scent diffuser. Many people have used this trick with a slow cooker, but people tend to forget that the Instant Pot is a multi-purpose cooker and has slow-cooker settings! Of course, you don't have to just use potpourri. You can add in citrus fruit skins, cinnamon sticks, essential oils, and many other things for your favorite fragrance.*

## Directions

1. Place potpourri and water into the metal liner of your Instant Pot. Press the Slow Cooker Low Heat button. Set the time for how long you want to use your IP for a potpourri diffuser.

## Ingredients

A bag of your favorite potpourri

4 cups of water

# GEL AIR FRESHENER

**Makes 6 (½-pint) mason jars**

*Air fresheners can be expensive, especially if you like having a really nice-smelling house or car. Well, we can officially solve that problem by making our own gel air fresheners! You can make them in any size container, including little mint tins. Best of all? They're so easy to make, and very cost effective.*

*Do you love using essential oils? Then you'll love doing this project!*

## Directions

1. Add water to your Instant Pot liner and press the Sauté button. Once the water looks like it wants to boil, press the Cancel button, and add in all of your ingredients.

2. Mix your ingredients well so as to not have any lumps. Pour contents into your storage containers. Allow to completely cool before adding lids. Once completely cool and at room temperature, cover with a piece of plastic food storage wrap and then place lid on top.

3. Whenever you're ready to use one, remove the plastic layer and enjoy!

## Ingredients

2 cups water

1 oz. unflavored gelatin powder

1 Tbsp. salt

5 drops green food coloring

15 drops lime essential oil

7 drops mint essential oil

6 half-pint mason jars, but any empty jars with lids and containers will work. Just make sure your lids have holes in them, or are lids that you can drill holes into.

# HONEY MINT LOZENGES

**Makes approximately 50 lozenges**

*Throat lozenges are really great to have on hand. Not only are they necessary when you have a cold and need something to soothe your throat from coughing too much, but sometimes your throat is just a little dry from allergies or anything else. It happens to all of us, and there's nothing better than a nice soothing lozenge to help "wet our whistle" a little. And I never knew how simple they were to make. The added bonus to this recipe is that it's not made with a ton of sugar. It's made with simple ingredients, starting with organic honey.*

## Directions

1. Add water and mint to pot and press Sauté button. Once water starts boiling, press the Cancel button and allow mint to steep in water for approximately 15–20 minutes.

2. Strain out the mint, and set mint-infused water to the side.

3. Add honey and ½ cup of the mint water that you made to your pot. Insert candy thermometer. Press the Sauté button and set time for 25 minutes. You want the thermometer to reach at least 280°F, but the goal is 300°F. It took me approximately 25–30 minutes to reach 300°F.

4. Once done, pour mixture onto a silicone mat. Allow to cool to where you can touch it. This will take approximately 15–20 minutes.

5. Pinch off a piece of mixture (about size of a nickel) and hand roll. Once rolled out, cover all pieces with arrowroot flour to stop them from sticking. Wrap each piece with wax paper and place in an airtight storage container.

## Ingredients

1½ cups of water
3 sprigs of mint on stem
16-oz. bottle of organic honey
Candy thermometer
½ cup arrowroot flour
Wax paper

# NUTRITIOUS PLANT FOOD SPRAY

**Makes 4 cups**

*Don't know what to do with your banana peels after making your delicious banana bread? Do I have a "solution" for you! Did you know that banana peels have many nutrients that are fabulous to feed your plants? Bananas provide potassium, calcium, phosphorus, manganese, and other nutrients that your plants will devour! Plus, it's cost effective and super easy to make!*

## Directions

1. Add banana peels and water into your Instant Pot liner. Close and lock the lid, and close the vent.

2. Press Pressure Cook button and set time for 7 minutes. Once 7 minutes is up, QPR.

3. Allow contents to cool completely. Remove banana peels and transfer liquid to spray bottle via a funnel.

## Ingredients

5 banana peels
4 cups water
Spray bottle
Funnel

*Tip:* You can also add ground-up eggshells to the water bottle. Make sure eggshells are completely dry. Place in food processor, and grind it up until the shells are in a powder form. Two or three eggshells will work perfectly.

# HOMEMADE PETROLEUM JELLY (WITHOUT THE PETRO)

**Makes 1 cup**

*Gone are the days of petroleum-based petroleum jelly! Now you can use this super-simple recipe to make your own. People use petroleum jelly for hair conditioner, hand salve, foot balm, lip moisturizer, and so much more than I can actually list. If you love your jelly, then you'll love how easy it is to make your own.*

## Directions

1. In a bowl (using double-boil method from page xi), add olive oil and beeswax. Stir occasionally until beeswax pellets have melted.

2. Once beeswax has completely melted, remove bowl from pot and pour contents into an airtight mason jar or other container.

## Ingredients

1 cup olive oil
¼ cup white beeswax pellets

# QUICK WOOD CHIP PREPARATION

**Makes 2 cups prepared wood chips**

*Everyone loves the amazing flavor profile that comes with smoking food; however, not everyone has the patience to wait for the wood to finish soaking. The suggested amount of time is traditionally 3–4 hours for wood chip smoking, and some people even recommend soaking the wood chips overnight. The biggest reason is make sure that the wood pieces are truly saturated. Thanks to the Instant Pot, we're going to cut that time down drastically! You can have 2 cups of wood chips ready for your smoker in less than 20 minutes!*

## Directions

1. Place water into your Instant Pot liner. Place wood chips into the steamer basket and place into your Instant Pot. Close and lock lid, and close the vent. Press Pressure Cook and adjust time for 3 minutes.

2. Once done, allow the wood to NPR for approximately 10–12 minutes to release the remaining pressure.

3. Remove steam basket, and your wood chips are ready to use!

## Ingredients

3 cups warm water
2 cups of wood chips (I love hickory)
Steamer basket

When I started thinking about the possibilities of different home and beauty items that you can make in the Instant Pot, my brain was reeling in awe. There are SO many things that you can make, and these projects are just the tip of the iceberg.

The best part of making your own products for your home is that you know you're making things that don't have harmful or harsh chemicals. You know exactly what's going into the products you're using, which is extremely beneficial if you're someone that has sensitive skin or allergies, or if you simply don't want certain types of chemicals and products in your home. Plus, these also make fabulous gifts for any birthday or holiday. These are amazing "Go To" things to make, and your friends and family members will know that they are made with love.

What I love about these tutorials is that they are all made with simple and real ingredients, they're not hard to make, and they're not extremely time consuming at all! These reasons alone check off many boxes that make me happy in wanting to make projects for my home.

All of these projects are simple to modify with whatever other ingredients, scents, colors, quantity, or shapes you like—it's all up to you! I'm just here giving you the backbone basics of what the possibilities are.

In making a lot of these products, we will be using the double-boil method that I described on page xi. Please take note: You will want to keep your eye open for the water level. You don't want your pot getting too low or having no water at all. You can cause damage to your Instant Pot if you run out of water. The Instant Pot has safety features involved for when it gets overheated; however, they are not 100 percent effective, and Instant Pot informs you of this. Take care of your Instant Pot, and your Instant Pot will take care of you.

# Homemade Beauty Products

# MOISTURIZING LIP BALM

**Makes about 12–14 lip tube containers, or 10–12 round lip balm containers**

*Who doesn't love an amazing lip balm? Take a look in your purse or backpack. How many tubes of lip balm do you have right now? See, everyone needs one or two in their arsenal. With this, you're going to be able to always have them on hand, and have extras to share for all of your friends that ask to borrow yours. You will be able to find beeswax pellets at any of your major craft stores; however, not all stores sell shea butter. I found that I was easily able to find this on Amazon, but many online retailers do sell this.*

*The quantity this makes depends on what you're using to put your lip balm in.*

## Directions

1. Use the double-boil setup that was described on page xi. Add 4 cups of water into pot liner and press the Steam button. Modify the time for as long as you need. I started with 20 minutes.

2. In a glass or metal bowl over your Instant Pot, add shea butter and coconut oil. Once the shea butter and coconut oil have melted, add in your beeswax.

3. Stir ingredients occasionally. Once everything has melded together, add vitamin E oil and essential oil. Mix well.

4. Using the plastic dropper, add your liquefied lip balm mixture into the containers. Allow 25–30 minutes to cool and solidify before using.

## Ingredients

4 cups water
2 Tbsp. shea butter
4 Tbsp. coconut oil
3 Tbsp. white beeswax pellets
1 Tbsp. vitamin E oil
10–15 drops of your favorite essential oil (optional)
Plastic dropper
Lip balm/lip tube containers

*Tip:* Want to make things more fun? Add in a little bit of your favorite lipstick color to add a splash of color and tint! You would add in your lipstick color once the beeswax has melted—lipstick doesn't take that long to melt. Stir the color into your mixture with a wooden craft stick or a plastic utensil.

# MINT-INFUSED LOTION BARS

**Makes approximately 10–12 lotion bars (depending on size of mold)**

*I have a bit of an infatuation with lotion bars. I don't mind buying lotion; however, I hate that the pump gets dry when you don't use it for a day or two. And I don't like how certain lotions still leave my skin feeling dry, or else are too thick and filmy. These lotion bars are simply fabulous. They're made with real ingredients that make your skin feel loved and hydrated.*

## Directions

1. Use the double-boil setup on page xi. Add 4 cups of water into pot liner and press the Steam button. Modify the time for as long as you need. I started with 20 minutes.

2. To your metal/glass bowl, add coconut oil and shea butter. Once melted, add beeswax and vitamin E oil. Stir occasionally.

3. Remove bowl from your Instant Pot once your ingredients have melted and have melded together. Add in sprigs of mint and allow to steep, like a tea bag, for 10 minutes. You have to keep the mixture in its liquid state, so you will have to alternate the bowl (on and off) over your Instant Pot to retain heat.

4. Remove mint from your melted lotion potion, and slowly ladle (or drip using a plastic eyedropper) into your molds for your lotion bars.

5. Allow 4–5 hours before removing from molds, or place in the refrigerator for 1 hour and then remove molds to help shorten the wait time.

## Ingredients

4 cups water
1 cup coconut oil
1 cup shea butter
1 cup white beeswax pellets
1 Tbsp. vitamin E oil
3 sprigs of fresh mint (on stem)
Silicone bar molds or other fun silicone molds

*Tip:* For visual fun, you can add in shreds of flowers or mint leaves to the bottom of the molds before adding your melted lotion potion. You can also use the peel of different citrus fruits and other fresh herbs. Rosemary and grapefruit are always a fabulous combination together.

# HAND SALVE

**Makes ½ cup**

*Hand salve is a little bit thicker than your traditional lotion. It uses beeswax to create a thick emollient, which surrounds the hands and then moisturizes the skin. Hand salves use all-natural ingredients that are known to heal and moisturize the skin. It's not recommended to use hand salve on your face, as it may clog pores. It is a gardener's best friend! Calendula oil is thought to have antifungal and antibacterial properties. Oil infused with calendula flowers has traditionally been used in hand salve creation. You will find it at most farm-supply stores and online without any problems.*

## Directions

1. Add 4 cups water into pot liner and press the Steam button. In a bowl (using double-boil method from page xi), add all shea butter and calendula oil. Once ingredients have melted, add in beeswax and rosemary essential oil.

2. Stir occasionally until all ingredients have melded together.

3. Remove bowl from on top of your Instant Pot, and pour liquid content into your favorite container to store. Allow 1 hour to cool before using. Use as needed for whenever your hands are feeling a little dry.

## Ingredients

4 cups water
2 Tbsp. shea butter
⅓ cup calendula oil
1½ Tbsp. white beeswax pellets
15 drops rosemary essential oil

# ALL-NATURAL DEODORANT

**Makes 4 tubes**

*If you're afraid of using store-bought deodorants or are tired of paying high prices for all-natural deodorants, then this is going to be your favorite project in this book! The initial cost of certain products can be expensive; however, once you add up all of your costs and do a breakdown of how many sticks of deodorant you can make, you'll be amazed at how much money you'll be saving in the end. Mango butter, like shea butter, is one of those ingredients that will be easier to find online than in a store. A lot of big health-food stores will have it available; however, if you're not located next to one, then let your mouse do the shopping!*

## Directions

1. Add 4 cups water into pot liner and press the Steam button. In a bowl (using double-boil method from page xi), add coconut oil, mango butter, beeswax, and vitamin E oil. Stir occasionally until all ingredients have melted.

2. Remove bowl from Instant Pot and add in baking soda, arrowroot, and essential oils. Stir until all ingredients have melded together thoroughly.

3. Pour deodorant mixture into your tubes. This will solidify pretty fast, so don't allow to cool to room temperature. I found a plastic eyedropper to be super useful.

## Ingredients

4 cups water
½ cup coconut oil
½ cup mango butter
½ cup + 1 tsp. white beeswax pellets
1 tsp. vitamin E oil
3 Tbsp. non-aluminum baking soda or cornstarch
½ cup arrowroot flour
15 drops essential oil (use your favorite—I'm partial to grapefruit and basil)
4 deodorant tubes
Plastic eyedropper

# PAIN-RELIEF CREAM

**Makes 1 cup**

*We all get those minor aches and pains that we could use a little help with. Just think about how much money is spent on over-the-counter pain-relief cream. Now you can make your own with ingredients that you can trust are all natural. You may be wondering what arnica oil is. It has long been used by many people who have suffered from arthritis and have looked for alternative ways to help control the pain. It's also been used for muscular and joint pain. The arnica plant is believed to have anti-inflammatory properties.*

## Directions

1. Add 4 cups water into pot liner and press the Steam button. In a bowl (using double-boil method from page xi), add coconut oil, shea butter, and beeswax. Heat and stir occasionally until melted.

2. Once melted, add in essential oils and arnica oil. Stir well.

3. Remove bowl from pot and pour contents into your favorite container to store. Allow to cool and solidify to room temperature before using.

## Ingredients

4 cups water
⅓ cup coconut oil
⅓ cup shea butter
⅓ cup white beeswax pellets
10 drops eucalyptus essential oil
10 drops peppermint essential oil
1 Tbsp. arnica oil

# BATH & SHOWER JELLIES

**Makes about 12 jelly "bars," depending on the size of your mold**

*This is one of those projects that you'll love making for your children. This is especially great to have on hand if you happen to have one of those kids who goes through gallons of liquid body wash and never really comes out clean. These are so colorful, fun to play with (so you'll be sure that your kid will come out clean), and a breeze to make. What can be better? Oh yeah, it'll save you body wash by the gallon! If you want to spice it up, you can add your favorite essential oils to make them smell all pretty.*

## Directions

1. Add 1½ cups water to your Instant Pot metal liner. Press the Sauté button and wait for water to gently boil. Once boil has been achieved, press the Cancel button and stop.

2. Gently add in and stir the gelatin, and mix until well dissolved. Be sure to pay attention to any lumps or bumps. We don't want any of those in our mixture.

3. Then add in your body wash, and gently mix so as to not cause any kind of bubbles. From there, I divided my mixture in half and added in the food coloring. I added 6 drops of blue to one and 6 drops of green to the other, and gently mixed.

4. Pour your mixture into your favorite silicone molds. Allow up to 24 hours to set, or place in the fridge to help set faster.

## Ingredients

1½ cups water
1 oz. unflavored gelatin powder
1 cup body wash
Blue and green food dye
Silicone molds

*Tips:* These store well in the fridge or freezer, since we are making them in batches. I made them into small squares because if you leave them in the bathtub or shower, then they will turn into gloop. However, once you're done with shower or bath, you can simply put it in a plastic storage container and place in the fridge to keep safe. I find smaller molds more convenient to use.

# ROSE PETAL BATH MELTS

**Makes about 14 small squares**

*People love adding calming and soothing elements to a long, relaxing hot bath. Between bubble baths and essential oils, people use all kinds of products when they want their skin to feel and smell amazing. If you love pampering your skin, then you need to make these rose petal bath melts. Your skin is going to feel so luxurious and supple. This recipe is flexible, so you can change up the base ingredients to whatever scents or floral arrays you care for. You can make these for yourself, or share the luxury with a friend who could use a little bit of relaxation.*

## Directions

1. Set up your Instant Pot for the double-boil method (from page xi). Place 2 cups of warm water into your Instant Pot liner. Press Sauté to start heat.

2. Add cocoa butter, shea butter, and coconut oil into bowl to melt. Once melted, add in beeswax. After the wax has been incorporated thoroughly, press the Cancel button to stop heat.

3. Add the minced rose petals into mixture, and then pour contents into your mold. I found a plastic eyedropper to be very useful.

4. Allow to cool and store in the fridge until you are ready to use them. These are heat sensitive, so you don't want to place them in any type of warm environment.

## Ingredients

2 cups warm water

¼ cup cocoa butter

¼ cup shea butter

1 tsp. coconut oil

1 tsp. beeswax pellets

¼ cup rose petals, minced

Silicone molds (you can also use the wax molds we used to make the scented wax melts)

Plastic eyedropper

# SHOWER LOOFAH WITH SOAP

*Makes 6 mini loofahs*

*Life is always better when it's conveniently simple, like it is with my shower loofah and soap idea. It takes soap on a rope to a completely different level—a more fun one! Now you can wash your body with your loofah and soap at the same exact time. You no longer have to worry about how much soap you need to use on your favorite loofah. You've always got the perfect amount!*

## Directions

1.  We are going to use the double-boil method (page xi) for this project. Prepare by adding 4 cups of water into the Instant Pot Liner. Shave your 4 bars of soap into a glass or metal bowl that you're placing on top of your IP, and then add in the 4 tablespoons of water. Press the Steam button and adjust the time for 25 minutes.

2.  Keep a wooden spoon or craft stick handy to stir your soap mixture as it melts. You are not going to get a super fluid soap melt. It's going to be just about as loose as body wash, maybe a little bit thicker.

3.  Once you've achieved this, pour the soapy contents into the muffin tins. Wait 1 minute to allow mixture to cool, and then gently press in the mini loofahs to spread the soap in. Don't press too hard, just firm enough to get soap stuck to the loofah.

4.  Place in the fridge to allow soap to cool and harden for about 30–40 minutes.

5.  You're ready to shower and start using your fabulous new the loofah!

## Ingredients

4 cups water + 4 Tbsp. warm water, *divided*
4 bars of your favorite soap
6 mini loofah sponges
Potato peeler
Muffin tin tray with 6 molds

When you think about DIY projects, turning on your Instant Pot may not exactly be your first thought; however, I'm excited to teach you to do exactly that!

Making DIY crafts or projects with your Instant Pot is going to be so much fun because it's opening up a whole new world of what you can do with your amazing appliance. Remember in the introduction where I said I wanted to encourage you to use the Instant Pot as you would your favorite wooden spoon in the kitchen—on a daily basis?

That's exactly what we're going to do! We're going to use our "wooden spoon" to make some super fun and familiar projects. I hope that by creating some (or all) of these projects, that you are inspired to make many other things and find more uses for your Instant Pot.

Let's get to crafting, shall we?

# DIY Projects

# TIE-DYE CLOTHES

**Makes 1 shirt; or you can do 2 at a time until you run out of liquid**

*Tie-dye clothes will never go out of style. The fashion seems to linger on from generation to generation. It's a great style; plus, it's a fun DIY project to do with the kids. Grab your Instant Pot and whatever article of clothing they want to tie-dye. Here's how I did this awesome shirt!*

## Directions

1. Fill your pot in between the ½ and ⅔ fill marks on the inside of your pot. Press Sauté normal mode to heat water, and then add your salt.

2. Once water is hot, add in your fabric dye. Add a lot of dye if you want a dark impression, or use less for lighter color tones. After rubber banding off the pieces of clothing in the pattern you want (I used the folded fan technique on mine—see below), then place the clothes or articles of clothing into your pot. Let set for at least 45 minutes. I rotated my shirt once in a while.

3. Rinse under cold water when done. Try to get out as much of the dye as you can. Remove rubber bands and allow to air-dry.

## Recipe Notes

Do not wash with other clothes for the first time. Wash by itself for its very first initial wash.

## Ingredients

Salt (read directions on your dye for amount to use)
RIT Teal fabric dye, available at craft stores
Rubber bands
White shirt

---

*Tip:* How to do a fan fold dye technique:

1. Lay your T-shirt on a flat surface and smooth out any wrinkles.

2. Starting from the bottom and working your way to the top, fold a 2-inch portion of the shirt up toward the neckline. Then move the 2-inch space and grab the shirt edges to create a fold in the opposite direction. You will continue this process of folding the shirt back and forth to make an accordion-style folded shirt.

3. With your rubber bands in hand, wrap them around the spots that you want in the different alternative color of staying white. I used a total of 8 rubber bands for my design.

# SILK-DYED EASTER EGGS

*Thanks to Jamela Porter from By-Pink.com for this great Instant Pot DIY! She figured out how to dye eggs with silk, and I knew I had to share it. You're about to make Easter a whole lot more fun. You're going to be the coolest and most hip parent for making this silk-dyed Easter eggs! However, I have some sad news: you cannot eat these eggs, because clothes are dyed with a different type of chemical than a food coloring agent, and it could make you seriously ill. To make these eggs, we are going to use the 5-5-5 method. Here's how to do it.*

## Directions

1. Wrap each egg in a piece of silk tie fabric. Use a rubber band and tie off the ends together like a tiny ponytail.

2. Place eggs into your pot. Fill with water and vinegar. Close lid and lock vent. Cook on high manual pressure for 5 minutes. Once done, allow to NPR for 5 minutes. QPR any remaining pressure. Carefully place eggs into ice bath for 5 minutes.

3. Once done, remove the pieces of fabric, and you will see a gorgeous design on your egg.

## Ingredients

1 dozen eggs

12 (3-inch) square cut scraps of fabric from silk ties (Must have enough to wrap around the egg)

12 rubber bands (ponytail holders work best)

2 cups of water

½ cup distilled white vinegar

1 big bowl of ice water

*Tip:* Make sure you have permission to cut up those beautiful silk ties. I purchased mine from the thrift store! The more colorful the tie and the brighter the pattern, the more beautiful the design will appear on your egg.

# THE BEST PLAY DOUGH EVER

*I remember that I used to love playing with play dough for many years! One of the things I love about play dough, besides the vibrant colors, is the fact that it makes for great sensory play. It's great for tactile stimulus and relieving stress. Who needs a stress ball when you have play dough that you can squeeze and pull your frustration out on? This recipe is fabulous; it will last a long time and makes really large batches. So if you have a birthday party coming up, then this is the perfect thing to make for everyone to have fun with! If you start to notice that your play dough is drying out just a little bit, add a bit of water and massage it in. It's brand new all over again.*

## Directions

1. Pour water and coconut oil into the metal liner of your Instant Pot. Press the Sauté button and wait for water to start heating. Once the water has heated, add all other ingredients. You can also add in your food coloring of choice to create whatever colors you want.

2. Be sure to continually stir this with a wooden spoon. This mixture will thicken fast, in less than 2 minutes from start to finish. Once your ball starts to form, press the Cancel button to stop the heating process. Remember, your pot will remain hot, so it will be best to remove from the heat once the ball of dough has started to form.

3. Place play dough onto parchment-paper-lined cookie sheet to cool. Allow about 1–2 hours before allowing your child, or yourself, to play with it.

## Ingredients

1 cup water
1 Tbsp. coconut oil
1 cup all-purpose flour
⅓ cup salt
2 tsp. cream of tartar
Food coloring
Parchment-paper-lined cookie
   sheet for cooling

*Tip:* It's best to add the food coloring into your play dough before it gets to the ball stage. You can manually knead the color in, but it will take a little bit longer to get the color just right and to get rid of the marbleized appearance. Add fewer drops of food coloring to create pastel colors and more drops of food coloring for more bold and traditional colored play dough.

# RECYCLED CRAYONS

*Do you ever get tired of buying countless crayons all the time when you're not even sure where they go? Somehow they always get broken or worn to down to these little nubs that no one wants to use anymore. Now, you can recycle those leftover crayon bits and transform them into more fun multicolored crayons. Recycling crayons is nothing new—but people have only recently begun to repurpose crayons in their Instant Pots. You don't need anything amazing for molds to put the broken crayons in. I cut up an old silicone brownie mold that I got tired of and used it.*

## Directions

1. Place 1 cup of water and trivet into your Instant Pot liner. Arrange all of your crayons into your molds. You don't have to have the crayons with the same depth as your mold. The wax will melt and fill up the crevices. Add just a little extra on the height.

2. Lightly cover your mold with foil; this will stop the water droplets from creating a splattered look on the back of your crayon. Close and lock lid and close your vent.

3. Press the Pressure Cook button for 2 minutes, and then QPR once done. Remove the lid and allow to cool for a few minutes before removing the molds from your Instant Pot.

4. Allow molds to cool for approximately 15–20 minutes, and then you should be able to pop them right out without any issues.

## Ingredients

1 cup water
A bunch of broken crayons
Silicone molds that will fit in your Instant Pot
A piece of foil
Trivet

27 July

even a long and
... day on the
open seas. There
big billowing wave
around us and
no where
dry land
that

# ANTIQUE PAPER

*This is such a fun project to work on, and the effects on the paper are so cool. You can do so much with this paper, including making a journal out of it. I love the aged effect it gives, and the parchment style and feel that you get when you cure the paper. You can send out fabulous invitations and letters to all of your friends, use it to create special handwritten menus or a treasure map, or add a little bit of a creepy feeling to Halloween festivities.*

## Directions

1. Place water and tea bags into your Instant Pot liner. Press the Sauté button, and wait for water to come to a light boil.

2. While waiting for water to boil, take 10 pieces of white paper and ball them up into wads. Place the wads of paper into your steamer basket.

3. Once your water has come to a boil, press the Cancel button to turn off, and remove pot from the machine. Allow hot tea water to cool for approximately 10 minutes. You want the water warm, and not extremely hot. If the water is too hot, it will deteriorate the paper.

4. Dunk your steamer basket of paper into the tea water, allow to sit for about 3–4 seconds, and then remove. Set the basket into your sink drain to allow excess water to be removed. Allow about 2 hours to dry.

5. Preheat oven to 200 degrees F. Slowly and gently, unfold your wads of paper and place on the cookie sheet. I was able to place 2 pieces of paper onto each cookie sheet. It's okay if you get tiny rips in the edges. That simply adds extra flair. Allow to dry in oven for approximately 5 minutes.

6. Repeat this process until all of your sheets of paper are dried.

## Ingredients

4 cups water
5 tea bags
10 pieces of plain white printer paper
Steamer basket
Cookie sheet

# SUMMER CAMP BRACELETS

*Oh, summer camp. How I wish I could go back and relive those amazing memories. Life was so much simpler back then. I only had to worry about if I had enough money to purchase snacks from the canteen and whether my mom left a few extra dollars for me with the counselors. Besides the food and friendships that I made at camp, it was also filled with arts and crafts projects. Do you remember making these types of bracelets? We thought that we were the most stylish people when we sported these and our macramé jewelry. So if you're ever looking for a rainy-day or snow-day project to do with your children, then move this right up to the head of the list!*

## Directions

1. Place 1½ cups of water and popsicle sticks into the metal liner of your Instant Pot. Put in no more than 20 popsicle sticks at a time for best results. Close and lock lid, and close the vent.

2. Press the Pressure Cooker button and adjust the time for 20 minutes. Once done, allow it to NPR.

3. Once pressure has been released, use a pair of tongs to remove the popsicle sticks. One by one, bend and form them into the inside of the mason jars. We want the sticks to dry to the shape of the jars! Drying time varies, but should be about 2–2½ hours.

4. Once they're done drying, you can wrap your favorite washi pattern tape around them. Don't have washi tape? You can always use different types of craft paints.

## Ingredients

1½ cups water
Popsicle sticks (15–20 at a time)
Mason jars or small glasses
Washi tape

# MAKE YOUR OWN MOD PODGE

**Makes 1 cup**

*Mod Podge is one of those fabulous crafting supplies that can be expensive, but it's SO much fun to use in lots of different crafting projects. I love Mod Podge so much that I actually have two projects that I'm sharing with you that use it: my Glitter Bowl (page 59) and my Clothespin Dragonflies (page 57), which we will get to soon enough! Most DIY Mod Podge recipes call for a few different things: water and glue (watered-down glue), or flour, water, and sugar. I took things a step further and used all of the ingredients above because I had the absolute best results and was extremely happy with the outcome! I hope you enjoy this recipe, and find tons of fun uses for it!*

## Directions

1. Add all ingredients into the Instant Pot liner, and press the Sauté button. With a whisk, gently mix ingredients together until well combined.

2. Continue to gently whisk your mixture until it just starts to slightly thicken. Be sure to immediately remove the metal liner from the machine to help stop the cooking process (don't forget to press the Cancel button, too).

3. Pour your hot Mod Podge mixture into a heat safe container and allow to cool to room temperature. Once cooled, you'll be able to start using it!

## Ingredients

½ cup all-purpose flour
1 cup water
¼ cup white granulated sugar
4 oz. clear glue
1 tsp. vinegar

*Tip:* Store in the fridge, and pull out to use as needed. This batch will last a full month! If you are going to use all of the Mod Podge for one project in one sitting, then you don't have to add the vinegar. Vinegar is a natural antifungal agent and inhibits mold growth from occurring.

# CLOTHESPIN DRAGONFLIES

*This one doesn't technically use the Instant Pot, but it shows a great idea of how to use your homemade Mod Podge! These magical dragonflies are simple to make and adorable to look at. I created some of these for my sister's room, to go with the magical unicorn on her wall. All she was missing was some glittery dragonflies to add a little extra special touch. We are going to be using our homemade Mod Podge recipe (page 55) for this project!*

## Directions

1. Add a thick layer of Mod Podge to your clothespins.

2. Pile a good layer of glitter onto each clothespin using the black foam brush. Once done, take a finger and lightly press the layer of glitter onto each clothespin to ensure it is in the Mod Podge. Allow 25–30 minutes to dry. With your black foam brush, add on an additional layer of Mod Podge over the glittered clothespin. This will add a lovely protective barrier ensuring that glitter will not flake off onto anything.

3. Allow your clothespins to dry for 2 hours. Take your strips of crafting ribbon, and pinch them in the middle. Place the middle into your clothespins. With a pair of scissors, cut angles from the tip toward the middle of the ribbon to create the double-wing effect. Place glue dots on the back, and turn any wall into a magical wall full of dragonflies.

## Ingredients

Mod Podge (page 55)
Clothespins (as many as you want to make)
Glitter (I used rose and green glitter)
2-inch pieces of crafting ribbon (the ones with metal strings to form)
Black foam brush
Glue dots

# MOD PODGE GLITTER BOWL

*This is another great example of a Mod Podge DIY project, and are you going to love the simplicity of this. We're going to make a fabulous glitter bowl. This one takes a lot of patience, as there are several layers of Mod Podge used in making the bowl. The bowl isn't meant to hold a drastic amount of weight, but if you're a crafter, then it's perfect for holding threads, buttons, and other lightweight items.*

## Directions

1. In a small bowl, add glitter and Mod Podge. Mix thoroughly using a wooden craft stick or plastic disposable utensil.

2. Blow up balloon to the size you think you might want your bowl. We are going to be using the bottom of the balloon as the form for our bowl. Place the other end of the balloon in the pitcher or bowl.

3. With the black foam brush, add your first layer of Mod Podge. You will be painting the design of the bowl. Don't worry about any imperfections with the outline. We will take care of that later. Allow your layer to dry for about 25–30 minutes.

4. You will be applying a total of 8–9 layers. Please wait for each layer to dry before adding a new layer. Once you add your final layer, allow your glitter bowl to dry overnight.

5. Once totally dry, pop your balloon with the scissors. With your scissors in hand, trim away any imperfections along the edges of your bowl. This bowl will lay flat once you add things into the middle, so you won't have to worry about it teetering around. This will surely add a little extra fabulousness to your room.

## Ingredients

2 tsp. glitter, your favorite color

¼ cup Mod Podge (page 55; you can always in a little extra if you want to add more layers)

1 latex balloon

Plastic pitcher or a bowl (this is to help hold the balloon while it dries)

Black foam paintbrush

Scissors

# DIY CLAY

- - - - - - - - - - - - - - - - - - - - - - - - - - - - - - - - - - - - - - - - - - - - - -

**Makes approximately 1 pound**

*While I was doing some research on the different things that I could try to make at home, I saw many people making salt clay projects, and that got me to wonder if there was a great clay material that we could make in the Instant Pot. Turns out, that there is! It's most commonly known as air clay. The ingredients are basic enough that you should have them in your house right now.*

## Directions

1. Place baking soda, cornstarch, and water into your Instant Pot liner. Press Sauté button.

2. You are going to be constantly stirring your ingredients together. You will do this until the mixture has achieved the consistency of thick mashed potatoes, immediately press the Cancel button and remove the pot from the machine and set to the side to allow to cool for a few minutes, until you are able to handle it.

3. Once you're able to touch it, wrap your dough with the damp towel and allow it to cool for approximately 15–20 minutes. Remove the towel and knead your dough to get rid of any residual stickiness. You can use a little bit of cornstarch for dusting.

4. You're now ready to create everything to your heart's desire! I used this dough to make necklace pendants.

## Ingredients

2 cups baking soda
1 cup cornstarch
1¼ cups water
Damp towel

# CRYSTALLIZED FLOWERS

*You're going to have so much fun with the next two projects. This crystal-making process has been around for a while, and almost every single science class has covered this topic; however, I still love the creativity and science behind it. This project is for borax-based crystals.*

## Directions

1. Place water into your Instant Pot liner and press Sauté button. Bring the water to a boil. Once boil has been achieved, add borax until it stops dissolving. There's no real measurement. You will notice that it'll start getting cloudy. Once the cloudiness happens, it means you're at the point to where it'll stop dissolving.

2. Press the Cancel button and remove pot from machine. Evenly distribute contents into mason jars. Tie a piece of string to the end of each bunch of artificial flowers, and attach to middle of a pencil.

3. Place flowers into jars and place pencil flat on top of the jars.

4. In about 2–3 hours, you will see that you have fabulous crystals on your flowers, adding so much charm to them!

5. Once you've achieved the amount of crystal formations on the flowers that you want, simply remove and place on paper towels to allow to air-dry. Before you know it, you'll have gorgeous crystal flowers to add a piece of charm to your home!

## Ingredients

6 cups water
4–5 cups borax
3 mason jars
3 bunches of artificial flowers (only works in small bunches—if the flower is big, then do it by itself)
3 pencils

# COLORFUL GEODES FOR KIDS

**Makes 3 geodes**

*The next thing you need to make are these fabulous geodes. Your kids are going to love helping you make these and watch them form right before their very eyes. This is very similar to the previous crystal flower project; the only real difference is that we are using pipe cleaners and food coloring to achieve this look. The different-colored pipe cleaners help to create a base internal color for your geode.*

## Directions

1. Place water into your Instant Pot liner, and press Sauté button. Bring the water to a boil. Once boil has been achieved, add borax until it stops dissolving. There's no real measurement. You will notice that it'll start getting cloudy. Once the cloudiness happens, it means you're at the point at which it will stop dissolving.

2. While waiting for water to boil, form half egg shapes with a couple of pipe cleaners of the same color. I used 2 pipe cleaners for each color.

3. Press cancel and remove pot from machine. Evenly distribute contents into mason jars. Then add your food coloring to each jar, one red, one green, and one blue. Use a spoon to distribute the color in each jar. Tie a piece of string to the end of each pipe cleaner.

4. Place pipe cleaners into jars, and place pencil flat on top of the jars.

5. In about 2–3 hours, you will see that you have fabulous crystals form on your pipe cleaners.

6. Allow 24 hours for your crystals to fully form on your pipe cleaners. Once done, remove pipe cleaners from solution and place on paper towels to allow to dry. I gave my geodes a full 24 hours to dry.

## Ingredients

6 cups water
4–5 cups borax
6 vibrant-colored pipe cleaners (I used 2 red, 2 green, and 2 blue)
6 drops of each food coloring to match pipe cleaners (red, green, and blue)
3 mason jars
3 pencils

# FLORAL BEESWAX BOWLS

*I use this beautiful beeswax bowl to hold small flowers around my desk and home. There's really no end to what you can use the Instant Pot for in making things for your home. These beeswax bowls add so much charm to any room. This is something that you can make for your friends and family members as gifts, and they will totally fall in love with it. I hope you enjoy this tutorial for an amazing project.*

## Directions

1. Using the double-boil method (page xi), add your beeswax pastilles to a glass or metal bowl. Add 4 cups of warm water to the Instant Pot liner, press the Steam button, and set the time for 30 minutes. To help with the melting process, stir occasionally to ensure your pastilles don't clump up and take longer to melt.

2. Once your wax has melted, we can begin to make the bowl! You do so by dipping your water balloon into the wax. Wait about 8–10 seconds to allow it to cool before dunking again. You will be doing this over and over again until you achieve the thickness that you want your bowl to be.

3. Allow your bowl to cool for about 1 minute. Use a glue stick to tack floral notions onto the side of your bowl(s).

4. Dip your bowls into the wax a couple more times to seal your notions in place. Allow your bowl to cool for 2–3 minutes, and then pop your water balloon over a sink.

5. With the paring knife, cut off the rough edges and shape a flatter bottom. You can also use a craft warming flat top to slowly melt the rough edges and flatten the bottom.

## Ingredients

White beeswax pellets (you will need enough to fill whatever bowl you're using halfway—it took me approximately 6 cups)

4 cups warm water

Water balloon (filled with water)

Glue stick

Mini floral notions (but you can decorate your bowl with whatever you want)

Sharp paring knife

# RETRO '80S COFFEE CUPS

*If I am anything, I am a supreme child of the '80s. That means I love everything nostalgic, vibrant shocking colors and patterns, video games, The Golden Girls, and watching movies on my VCR, probably movies that I never returned to the video rental place. That's what inspired me to create these coffee cups . . . with nail polish. Yes, you heard me right!*

## Directions

1. Place 6 cups of warm water into your Instant Pot liner, and press the Sauté button to get your water extremely hot, but not boiling.

2. Once your water is super hot, press the Cancel button.

3. Open your nail polish and make scattered stark line designs on the water. Once you like what you see, dip your coffee cup in at an angle and pull out slowly. You'll notice how the nail polish wraps around the cup as you push it in the water.

4. Place your coffee cup upside down to cool and air-dry. Repeat this process for each coffee cup you make.

5. Once finished, drain the water from your Instant Pot, and use nail polish remover on a washcloth or towel to remove any nail polish residue from your pot. Once nail polish has been removed, wash with warm soapy water.

6. Your Retro '80s coffee cups are ready for you to enjoy your next cup of strong brew while rocking out to the Bangles while wearing multicolored bangles.

## Ingredients

6 cups warm water

Vibrant nail polish (the more colorful, the better!)

White coffee cups or mugs

Nail polish remover, to help with the cleanup

*Tip:* I definitely recommend washing these by hand, as you don't want your design to get flaked off by the harsh chemicals of a dishwasher. These coffee cups will last you for years to come!

# RUBBERIZED EGGS EXPERIMENT

*This is something just so cool that I had to share with you. Your kids are going to love the outcome of this science experiment! I used the Instant Pot because of the constant temperature environment that doesn't fluctuate at harsh levels. For this, we will be using the Yogurt setting with less heat. Let's go have fun!*

## Directions

1. Place an egg into each of your 3 containers and cover with vinegar. Add 4 drops of red food coloring to one container, 4 drops of blue food coloring to the second, and leave the third plain.

2. Add 4 cups of warm water to the Instant Pot liner, and press Yogurt button with less heat for 24 hours. Seal jars finger tight (not too tight!), and place into the Instant Pot.

3. After 24 hours have passed drain the vinegar from each jar. Take each egg and gently rub the egg under cold running water. You will see that the eggshell has almost disintegrated, and small circular motions of your fingertips rub the exterior shell off. You now have a "rubber" egg.

## Notes

Please note that this is a chemical reaction that has happened with the shell proteins and the acidic vinegar. The egg is still raw in the middle. Once you're done playing with your rubber egg, make sure to wash your hands well.

When you're completely done with your egg, give it a good squish! You'll see that you're left with only the outer layer. Now you have a real reason to wash your hands.

## Ingredients

3 eggs
3 (½-pint) mason jars or containers with lids
White vinegar
Red and blue food coloring
4 cups warm water

# EDIBLE WATER PEARLS

**Makes 6 cups**

*Water beads are so much fun to play around with, but unfortunately they're not very eco friendly and can be harmful if swallowed. I've translated this idea to the Instant Pot and we're going to be using edible tapioca pearls. Let's get started and have fun!*

## Directions

1. Add 2 cups of warm water to your Pyrex dish and add sugar. Stir well until dissolved. Then add in your tapioca pearls.

2. Place 2 cups of warm water to your Instant Pot liner and place trivet into base. Place your Pyrex dish onto the trivet. Close and lock lid and close vent. Press the Pressure Cook button and adjust time for 7 minutes.

3. After time has finished, NPR for 10 minutes and then release any remaining pressure. Remove lid and remove trivet with Pyrex dish on it. Stir contents well and allow to cool for 30 minutes.

4. Empty your tapioca pearls into the colander and run under cold water to prevent any further "cooking" action from happening.

5. Divide the tapioca pearls evenly across the 3 jars. Add 6 drops of food coloring to each jar and then fill with cold water. I used green, blue, and yellow food coloring. Seal the jars and place in the fridge overnight.

6. The next day, you wake up to these gorgeous colored tapioca pearls, and your little one is going to love playing with them. You can let them eat these little water beads without any fear of them consuming anything toxic.

## Ingredients

4 cups warm water, *divided*
7-cup Pyrex dish
¼ cup granulated sugar
½ cup large tapioca pearls
Trivet
Colander
3 pint-sized mason jars with lids
Food coloring

## Notes

The color of these water beads will last for about 2 days, if they are mixed with the other color beads. They will last longer in the fridge, so be sure to store them there when not in use.

# BIRDSEED WREATHS

**Makes 4 mini wreaths or 2 large wreaths**

*My grandparents, aunt, and mom loved wildlife so much. They especially loved bird-watching. Their yards would always be littered with birds of all varieties, and they had just about every single bird feeder that you can think of, including condos for birds. I'm not kidding. Birdseed wreaths are just another part of what could always be found in my family's yards. In their honor, I decided to use the Instant Pot to make a couple.*

## Directions

1. To your Instant Pot liner, add: water, gelatin, flour, and corn syrup. Press the Sauté button. Stir ingredients well until heated. You want to heat ingredients until you get a nice hot glue working. You don't want to boil the mixture. Just thicken it. Once glue consistency has been achieved, press the Cancel button to stop it from continuing to cook.

2. Add in your birdseed and mix well.

3. Spray your pans down with the nonstick spray and fill each pan with the birdseed mixture. Be sure to pack it in and don't be afraid of pressing the seed mix hard into the mold.

4. Once done, allow 24 hours to cool and solidify.

5. Remove birdseed wreaths from molds and tie a ribbon through each loop. Hang your beautiful new birdseed wreaths all over your yard for the birds to enjoy.

## Ingredients

1 cup warm water
.5 oz. unflavored gelatin powder
1½ cups flour
6 Tbsp. corn syrup
7 cups birdseed
Nonstick cooking spray
4 mini Bundt pans or 2 large (9-inch) Bundt pans
Heavy-duty crafting ribbon

There are tons of tips for the Instant Pot circulating, but I'm pretty positive that you didn't know that you could use it to make these awesome food products!

I am going to show you how to make real things that you can eat and drink, just by making small modifications. Did you ever want to cook corn on the cob to pure perfection? Or maybe you've wanted to try your hand at making your own cream cheese?

You can do all this and more, with everyday ingredients that you should already have in your house, or that you can get from any store.

I hope you enjoy this section as much as I enjoyed writing it all up!

# Foodie Hacks

# CORN ON THE COB

*It can be such a pain to have to strip the husks off the cobs, and then have to cook sweet corn in a big pot of water, steaming up your home. No one wants to have to worry about that, right? This is going to make your life so much easier.*

1. Grab 5–6 ears of corn, in the husk. Cut the bottoms and tops off.

2. Place them in the pot and add 2 cups of water. Cook on high manual pressure for 3 minutes, and then QPR.

3. Allow the cobs of corn to cool before serving. Now the corn will literally squeeze right out of the husk—no need for shucking!

4. Some people like to shuck the corn and then cook just the cobs in the Instant Pot. If this is the case, you can add 1½ cups water, ½ cup milk, and ½ stick of salted butter to the Instant Pot with the same amount of cooking time.

5. No matter how you end up cooking your corn in the pot, it turns out simply amazing.

# RIPEN BANANAS IN A FLASH

*Are you in need of ripened bananas to make your famous banana bread right now, and not in 3–5 days? I have the best solution for you! Just put them in your Instant Pot. Yes, it's that easy.*

1. Put as many bananas as you need into your pot, skin on.
2. Add 1½ cups of water. Lock your lid and close your vent. Cook on high manual pressure for 2 minutes and then QPR the pressure out of it. Carefully remove bananas and allow to cool before peeling. It's like pure magic!

# EASY VANILLA EXTRACT

**Makes 6 cups**

*I'm known for my chocolate chip cookies. I make so many batches that I keep vanilla extract companies going strong—but I finally decided to make my own. I didn't know how easy it was to make, until I saw my fellow pot heads in the Instant Pot Facebook Group posting about how they made it. I was floored, and couldn't wait to make my own! This stuff is of primo quality, and makes the most amazing chocolate chip cookies!*

*As with the warning I mentioned previously, Instant Pot does not condone the usage of alcohol in it's device as it releases trace amount of fumes. Please be sure to make this in a well ventilated area and keep away from any type of open flames.*

## Directions

1. Split the vanilla beans in half lengthwise.

2. Divide the vanilla beans and vodka between the 3 jars.

3. Seal the jars and add to your pot. Place the lids on the jars and seal finger tight. Set the Instant Pot's trivet in the bottom of the insert. Place the jars on the trivet with equal space around them.

4. Add the water to the Instant Pot, close lid and vent, and cook on high pressure for 45 minutes. Allow your pot to NPR when done.

5. Your jars will be HOT! Remove with tongs and place on towel or a cooling rack, if you wish.

6. Enjoy! Use immediately or store for whenever you need it. This will store and last for years to come!

## Ingredients

6 vanilla beans, preferably grade B
6 cups vodka (cheap is fine!)
Trivet
3 (16-oz.) glass jars with lids
1 cup water

# INFUSED OLIVE OILS

*I love adding different flavors to my food when preparing them. Whether you want to splash it over a mixed greens salad, to sauté food, or to use it as a finishing touch over your freshly cooked pasta, infused olive oils can add such robust flavor.*

*My favorite types of oils to use are rosemary and thyme, but you can use whatever herbs you wish—or, you can mix it up and use your favorite variety.*

## Directions

1. Place rosemary in your empty glass bottle and fill with olive oil. Place top on bottle.

2. Place water inside your Instant Pot, and place bottle of oil in it.

3. Press Yogurt function, Less Heat. Leave in the water bath overnight or for approximately 8 hours.

4. Once done, remove bottle from water. Your oil will be ready to go! For best results, leave bottle in the pot for 12 hours.

## Ingredients

3–4 sprigs of dried rosemary or thyme

1 bottle of olive oil (I prefer extra-virgin, but any will do)

1 glass olive oil bottle with top

6 cups warm water

*Tip:* If you don't want to make these in large glass bottles, you can make them in small batches in mason jars. This way you can make them as gifts, or try out different flavors.

# DETOX TEA

**Makes approximately 1 gallon**

*This recipe was handed down to me from a pastry chef in a restaurant that I used to work in many moons ago. As soon as one person coughed or sneezed in the restaurant, she was sure to start a great big pot of her "Witch's Brew." We all happily drank it because it just makes you feel so much better.*

## Directions

1. Add all of the ingredients to your Instant Pot, except the honey.

2. Fill your IP Liner with water up to the ½ mark.

3. Place your pot inside the Instant pot, and lock the lid. Close the vent. Place on High Manual Pressure for 15 minutes and let it NPR.

4. Release the remaining steam and remove the lid.

5. Strain everything through a colander to separate the tea from the solids, then add in the honey and stir until it is dissolved. This is great chilled as well.

## Notes

Be sure to strain the liquid from the ingredients if storing in the fridge. You've cooked out all of the important properties that you want from it, so place it in your compost pile.

## Ingredients

2 oranges (cut into halves)
2 lemons (cut into halves)
1 bunch of parsley (rinsed, and left whole on stem)
3 celery stalks (cut into thirds)
½ inch ginger root (cut in half)
Water
½ cup Turkish honey (normal honey is fine, too)

# CREAMY ALMOND MILK

**Makes about 1 quart**

*I'm not lactose intolerant, but I do love the great taste of a cold glass of almond milk. I had no idea how easy it was to make and modify to my own flavor profile liking. Example: You can add in vanilla extract, almond extract, or other fabulous flavors.*

## Directions

1. Place raw almonds into your pot. Cover almonds with about an inch of water. Lock lid and close vent. The closed vent is to ensure nothing gets in. Remember, no pressure is created at all. But for safekeeping, release any stored pressure that there might be.

2. Press the Yogurt button with Less Heat (not normal or high). Set time for 8 hours. Allow the almonds to soak overnight.

3. Drain almonds and rinse under cold running water.

4. Add almonds and 2 cups of water into a blender, and blend for 2 minutes.

5. With either a nut bag or cheesecloth over a bowl or a pitcher, pour in the almond mixture. Twist and close cheesecloth/nut bag around the almond mixture and squeeze as much as you can. You will get about 2 cups of almond milk.

6. Store in a glass container, and it will last for at least 3–4 days. You can add any type of sweetener to the milk if you wish to do so.

## Ingredients

1 cup raw organic almonds

2 cups water + more for soaking almonds (filtered water is best)

1 fine mesh nut bag or cheesecloth

# SILKY CASHEW MILK

**Makes about 1 quart**

*After making both almond milk and cashew milk, I've learned that I'm more partial to cashew milk. It's very silky and smooth and has a lot of flavor. In fact, I love making a great latte with it and don't even need to add any sweetener to it.*

## Directions

1. Place raw cashews into your pot. Cover cashews with about an inch of water. Lock lid and close vent. The closed vent is to ensure nothing gets in. Remember, no pressure is created at all. But for safekeeping, release any stored pressure that there might be.

2. Press the Yogurt button with Less Heat (not normal or high). Set time for 8 hours. Allow the cashews to soak overnight.

3. Drain cashews and rinse under cold running water.

4. Add cashews and 2 cups of water into a blender, and blend for 2 minutes. Add 2 more cups of water, and blend for 20–30 seconds.

5. With either a nut bag or cheesecloth over a bowl or a pitcher, pour in the cashew mixture and strain.

6. Store in a covered glass container, and it will last for at least 3–4 days. You can add any type of sweetener to the milk if you wish to do so. Vanilla extract and honey are always great additions!

## Ingredients

1 cup raw unsalted cashews

4 cups filtered water, plus more for soaking cashews

1 fine mesh nut bag or cheesecloth

# LIMONCELLO

**Makes 3 pints**

*Limoncello is an Italian lemon liqueur that is mostly produced in the southern portion of Italy. Once made, Limoncello has a milky/cloudy appearance, which is due mostly to the essential oil droplets that are pulled from the lemon's skin during the Limoncello-making process. This super bright and delicious liqueur is easy to enjoy.*

*As with the warning I mentioned previously, Instant Pot does not condone the usage of alcohol in it's device as it releases trace amount of fumes. Please be sure to make this in a well ventilated area and keep away from any type of open flames.*

## Ingredients

10 organic lemons
750 mL bottle of vodka
3 widemouthed pint jars
2½ cups water
Trivet
2 cups simple syrup (page 107)

## Directions

1. Shave lemons with vegetable peeler or very thin knife. We do not want any of the white pith of the lemon, as that is the bitter part. We just want the outermost lemon skin. Divide the lemon shavings equally among the pint jars.

2. Divide the vodka between the three jars. Leave about a 1-inch space at the top of the jar. We don't want to overfill it, and we will need that extra space. You will still have extra vodka left over. Throw the remainder in the freezer and make yourself a cocktail with it later.

3. Pour 2½ cups of water into the metal liner of the Instant Pot, and place trivet into bottom.

4. Place lids onto pint jars, but be sure that the lids aren't on too tight. Put them on loosely, finger tight. Please do not use the two-piece canning-jar lids. Use normal lids. If you use canning lids, the sealing lids will seal on you during the resting process.

5. Place jars onto trivet. Close and lock lid, and turn the vent to the closed position. Press the Pressure Cook button, and adjust time for 30 minutes. Once done, press the Cancel button and allow to NPR. We don't need the warmer on.

6. Remove the lid from your Instant Pot and allow the jars to stay in the pot overnight. This will allow it to come to room temperature and allow the lemon peels to marinate in the vodka. The jars will be *extremely* hot, so please use caution if you are picking one up to see what it looks like. However, if you do pick up a jar, you will notice that it is bubbling. This is a natural process to have happen.

7. Let the jars rest overnight, and the next day strain your vodka into a big bowl. Take the simple syrup, and pour over the lemon peels in the jars. We just want to help rinse off any extra vodka remnants and flavor. Strain the syrup into the bowl of lemony vodka. You now have Limoncello!

8. Using a funnel, pour your Limoncello into your favorite containers and chill. Serve and enjoy! You can store this tasty beverage in the fridge for up to 3 months!

# GUMMY WORMS

**Makes about 24 worms if using the gummy worm mold**

*This recipe is a prime example of how I want people to use the Instant Pot as a daily kitchen tool and to create super fun things—like these gummy worms! You can change up the flavors and use whatever type of fun molds you want to use, or you can even pour the mixture on a cookie sheet and use cookie cutters to create your own fun adult-sized gummies. If you have children, they're going to love these! If you don't, then you'll be able to enjoy them even more.*

## Directions

1. Place water, Jell-O, and gelatin into your pot. Press sauté normal mode. Stir ingredients until dissolved.

2. You have to keep a close eye on this! You want it to just where the liquid starts boiling. Once it starts boiling, immediately remove the pot from the machine and set to the side. You don't want to overcook your mixture. Also, don't forget to press the Cancel button after removing the inner pot.

3. Transfer liquid to the worm mold with the plastic dropper. Allow liquid to cool for 15–20 minutes. You will notice it starting to firm. If you don't have any patience, you can always place the mold into the freezer or the fridge to help it set faster.

## Ingredients

1 cup water (filtered is best)
3-oz. package of Jell-O, flavor of
   choice (I used lime for the worms)
.75 oz. unflavored gelatin powder
Worm silicone mold
Plastic dropper

# COTTAGE CHEESE YOU'LL LOVE

**Makes 2 cups**

*Cottage cheese is one of my favorite foods to enjoy with sliced bananas, pineapple chunks, or mandarin orange segments on top. In fact, my whole family loves cottage cheese. Making cottage cheese is such an easy process—you literally need only four common household ingredients, and you're set to go on your merry little cottage-cheese-making way!*

## Directions

1. Pour the skim milk into your Instant Pot and press the Sauté button. You want to heat your milk to around 120 degrees F.

2. Once you've reached that temperature, press cancel and remove the pot from the machine. Slowly add in your vinegar, and gently stir the mixture for about 2 minutes. You will see that the curd will separate from the whey.

3. Cover your mixture and allow to sit at room temperature for at least 30 minutes. Try not to go beyond the 30 minutes, as I've noticed that the curds get really hard and tight, which isn't so enjoyable.

4. Pour the mixture into a colander lined with cheesecloth and strain and drain for 5–6 minutes. Then you want gather the edges of the cheesecloth into a bundle, and then rinse the curds under cold water for 3–5 minutes or until the curd is completely cooled. Be sure to squeeze and move the mixture while you're doing this.

5. Once completely cooled, squeeze the curds as dry as possible and transfer to a medium bowl. With a wooden spoon, add salt and stir while trying to break up all the curds. Finally, add in your heavy cream and mix well. Place in the fridge, and allow to sit for 30–45 minutes before eating.

## Ingredients

1 gallon pasteurized skim milk (I used FairLife)
¾ cup white vinegar
Colander
Cheesecloth
1½ tsp. kosher salt
½ cup heavy cream

DIY CRAFTS & PROJECTS FOR YOUR INSTANT POT

# FRESH CREAM CHEESE

**Makes 16 ounces**

*Just like cottage cheese, cream cheese is easy to make at home, especially with the help of your handy-dandy Instant Pot. Life doesn't get much better when you have homemade cream cheese readily available at your disposal. If you have my other cookbook, then you'll love using this to make my delicious pizza dip recipe!*

## Directions

1. Add milk to your Instant Pot and press the Sauté button. Wait until your milk starts to lightly simmer.

2. Once the light simmer has been achieved, slowly add in your lemon juice 1 tablespoon at a time. Be sure to gently stir your mixture while adding lemon juice at 1-minute intervals. During this process, you will notice the milk separating into curds, and a yellowish hue will appear. This is natural and is supposed to happen!

3. Line your colander with a piece of cheesecloth, and strain the whey from the curds. Allow the curds to cool for approximately 20 minutes.

4. Place the curds into a food processor, add salt, and pulse until smooth and creamy. This will take approximately 5 minutes. If you happen to notice that your cream cheese is a little bit on the gritty side, keep on pulsing and add a pinch more salt.

## Ingredients

4 cups whole milk
2–3 Tbsp. lemon juice
¼ tsp. kosher salt
Colander
Cheesecloth

# DISTILLED WATER

*Yes. You can actually make distilled water with your Instant Pot! Distilled water is great for so many different purposes for your home. The distillation process helps to remove impurities form the water. It's perfect for using in your iron, refilling your car battery, in your humidifier, and if you're lucky to have one, even your cigar humidor. You're about to call me crazy for what I'm going to have you do, but it's such a fun little hack.*

## Directions

1. Remove the venting knob on top of your Instant Pot lid. Just pull up, and it'll slide right off.

2. Add 1 gallon of water into the Instant Pot liner. Close lid and lock in place. Place one end of the vinyl tubing onto the metal piece sticking out of the vent hole and the other end to a heat-safe container.

3. Press the Steam button, and adjust time to 25 minutes. Watch your water steam! 20–25 minutes should be plenty of time to distill your water. Check your water level at about the 20-minute mark, as boiling times vary at different elevations.

## Ingredients

1 gallon of tap water
Food-grade heat-safe vinyl tubing, approximately 2½–3 feet long and ⁵⁄₁₆-inch diameter
Heat-safe container

*Tip:* Word of caution—the tubing and heat-safe container will be extremely hot, so please do not handle with bare hands. Even when the process is done, use oven-safe mitts to handle everything.

# COFFEE

**Makes 6 cups**

*Did your K-Cup machine break? Did you lose your French press? No worries—Instant Pot is here to save the day! The coffee comes out simply fabulous and full of that essential caffeine that helps run the world.*

## Directions

1. Add 6 cups of water to your Instant Pot liner. Press the Sauté button to start getting the water hot.

2. Fill the diffuser with your favorite coffee, and lock the diffuser in place.

3. Place the diffuser into the water. Close and lock the lid, and close your vent. Press the Cancel button to stop the sauté action. Press the Pressure Cook button and adjust the time to 4 minutes. Once cycle has completed, QPR all pressure out of it and ladle into your coffee cup.

## Ingredients

6 cups water

1 big loose-leaf metal tea diffuser that interlocks, approximately 4 oz. in size

Favorite ground coffee

# EASY *DULCE DE LECHE*

**Makes 14 ounces**

*There is nothing more satisfying than the taste of fresh* dulce de leche *made from sweetened condensed milk. This is another secret recipe hack that is shockingly simple. You're going to love how easy this is. The end result after cooking? A rich decadent caramel sauce that you can't stop eating.*

## Directions

1. Add 3 cups of warm water into your Instant Pot liner and insert trivet. Open your can of sweetened condensed milk, and be sure to remove paper label from the outside. Place a piece of foil on top of the can to stop condensation from entering.

2. Close and lock lid and close vent on lid. Press the Pressure Cook button for 45 minutes and allow it to fully NPR.

3. Remove lid and allow can to cool for a few minutes before removing from your IP. Remove can with a hand towel.

4. With a spoon, stir your *dulce de leche*. It's going to appear lumpy, but I promise you . . . stir it with your spoon, and the lumps will disappear completely.

## Ingredients

3 cups water
Trivet
1 (14-oz.) can sweetened condensed milk
1 piece of foil

# CITRUS-SPICED MAPLE SYRUP

**Makes 2 cups**

*This is such an amazing fall-weather treat to spice up maple syrup. This will make brunch even more amazing while enjoying a stack of your favorite waffles and sipping on a mimosa or a yummy Bloody Mary.*

## Directions

1. Add 1½ cups water to your Instant Pot liner and place trivet at the base.

2. Place all ingredients into mason jar, and seal lid finger tight. Don't seal the lid too tight.

3. Press the Pressure Cook button for 10 minutes. Once the cycle is complete, QPR all pressure. Press the Cancel button to prevent the warming cycle from staying on.

4. Remove lid, and allow syrup jar to cool for 15–20 minutes before removing.

5. Once cooled, open lid and remove rinds and cinnamon stick.

## Ingredients

1½ cups water
Trivet
1 cinnamon stick
Rinds of 2 mandarin oranges
2 cups pure maple syrup
1 pint-sized mason jar with lid
Trivet

## Recipe Note

This will store well in the refrigerator for up to two weeks, in a sealed air-tight container. So, I recommend having brunch every day!

# SIMPLE SYRUP

**Makes 3 cups**

*Simple syrup is one of those products that you'll probably wind up using more often than you think, especially if you love a great cocktail like a mint julep or Moscow Mule. I see this stuff being sold in grocery stores everywhere, and I always laugh when I see someone about to buy it . . . and then I tell them how to easily make it at home. So here's the most simple recipe for simple syrup that you're going to need to make if you want to make that fabulous Limoncello recipe (page 91).*

## Directions

1. Place water into your Instant Pot liner and press the Sauté button to heat water. Once you see that the water has come to a boil, add in your sugar.

2. Stir your mixture until all sugar has dissolved. Once sugar has been dissolved, boil for an additional 5 minutes.

3. Once 5 minutes has passed, press the Cancel button and remove pot from the machine so it doesn't continue to cook your simple syrup. Allow 15–20 minutes to cool before placing into a container to use.

## Ingredients

1½ cups water
1½ cups granulated sugar

# Hints, Tips, and FAQs

I hope these projects have inspired you to not be afraid of your Instant Pot, and to keep on using it for many other recipes you find or ones that you create yourself.

Questions will probably pop up, though. So, you followed my directions exactly, and you didn't get the same outcome that I did. We have to try to diagnose what happened along the process—there could just be something small that affected the results, or maybe it wasn't a recipe that you were having an issue with, but the Instant Pot itself. Well, let me see if I can help!

**1. Oh no! I poured liquid into my Instant Pot, and now it's all over the counter.**

Okay, so you forgot to the metal pot inside before pouring in your contents. *Always* double-check that your pot is in your machine before adding ingredients for a recipe. Does this mean that it's the end of the road for your machine? No, not always. Clean it up really well and allow it to fully dry before trying to plug in and use again.

**2. My Instant Pot has been on for over 20 minutes, and it still hasn't come up to pressure. It's just hissing away and steam is coming out.**

This can happen for a couple of reasons.

1. Did you move the vent to the closed position on your lid? If you didn't, no pressure will build up. The steam will just continue to come out of the vent.
2. Did you put frozen food into the pot? If you did, it will take the pot longer to come to pressure, because it is extra cold. It takes a while to get the right temperature to make the steam pressure that is required to get your pot to pressurize.
3. Check your pressure pin on the pot and make sure nothing is clogging the hole. If you're not properly cleaning your machine or giving basic maintenance, then it can get clogged and the pin will not be able to pop up. Pressurized steam will continue leaving the hole, and your machine will never come up to pressure.

4. You forgot to put your silicone ring back into the lid of your pot. This happens more often than you think—if you're cleaning your silicone ring after each usage, you can sometimes forget to put it back in.

5. Let's talk about your machine just not coming to pressure as fast as you thought it would. This can happen from putting in too much liquid into your pot. The more ingredients and liquid that are added into your pot, the longer it will take to come to pressure.

## 3. I got a burn notice on my machine. What did I do wrong?

There's a few things that could have gone awry here, but don't fret just yet.

1. You put dairy products into your Instant Pot while cooking. There are plenty of recipes that include dairy products like milk, heavy cream, and cheese. These are more dense than other liquids like stock and water. So they will stay close to the bottom of the pot, where the heating element is, and the bottom of the pot will start to get a little bit of a charring effect. For the most part, always add dairy in last. That is the general rule of thumb.

2. You didn't have enough liquid in your pot, or you used ingredients that are just too dense, such as crushed tomatoes, tomato sauce, etc.

3. Sometimes it is a user error. If you're following along with a recipe that you found online or in a cookbook, follow the order of ingredients. Cooking in your Instant Pot has a lot to do with layering ingredients in just the right way to make it work. Example: pasta dishes will always have pasta added in last, unless you're making mac and cheese. This is different because you're just cooking pasta in water, and adding other things to it. We spend a lot of time formulating recipes and how we can make them work in the Instant Pot. We make mistakes, but we fix them so other people can enjoy them as we do.

4. Did you put too much time on the cooking timer? Always double-check the amount of time you press for each recipe.

## 4. I want to make a recipe, but I'm not sure how much liquid to put into my pot.

Well, we've all been there! I definitely recommend starting off with 1 cup of liquid. Sometimes you'll need more, but that comes with trial and error cooking in your pot. Once you've become more familiarized with the cooking process, how to handle liquids for various dishes will become second nature.

## 5. My instant Pot smells so bad. How can I get rid of the smell?

There are a lot of things you can do.

1. One of the first things that I like to do is have two different sealing rings for the lid on hand. I use one for savory cooking and the other for my sweets cooking.
2. Cook a couple of russet potatoes in your pot, with the skin on. The skin of the potatoes helps to absorb the smell from the rings. I came across this by accident! You can cook the potatoes on High Manual Pressure for at least 4 minutes.
3. A lot of people wash their rings in the dishwasher or soak them in hot soapy water.
4. Some people swear by throwing in a cup of water with a couple of lemons cut in half. Put it on High Manual Pressure for 5 minutes, and the smell is gone.

## 6. My recipe is taking longer to cook than yours did!

That's to be expected. We all live at different levels of elevation. The higher your elevation, the longer it will take to come to pressure. This is also true with baking. While it can take me 2 hours to let my yeast dough rise, it could take you 2½ hours. Don't be afraid to put it back in your pot for a few more minutes! Here's a great cheat sheet to help with cooking times.

| If your home elevation is above . . . | increase by . . . | or multiply time by . . . |
|---|---|---|
| 3,000 feet | 5% | 1.05 |
| 4,000 feet | 10% | 1.1 |
| 5,000 feet | 15% | 1.15 |
| 6,000 feet | 20% | 1.2 |
| 7,000 feet | 25% | 1.25 |
| 8,000 feet | 30% | 1.3 |
| 9,000 feet | 35% | 1.35 |
| 10,000 feet | 40% | 1.4 |

## 7. I have so much liquid coming out of my vent when depressurizing it!

This tends to happen when you overfill your pot. It'll spew ingredients, juices, sauces, and food particles if you're trying to do a QPR when a recipe has finished. If you have a lot of liquid in your pot because you're making a big batch of soup, then slowly and gently QPR. You don't have to turn the valve to the vent open all the way. Put on a silicone oven mitt, and slowly turn the vent open a little bit at a time. This way not everything will come rushing out. I say to use a silicone oven mitt because steam can shoot through a cloth one.

## 8. Is an Instant Pot expensive?

In my opinion, they're not that expensive. I use mine very often. Many places have them on sale through the year, and the holidays are the perfect time to snag some amazing deals. You will probably have some thrift luck at a yard sale or a Goodwill store. Many people have found them there at a greatly reduced price. Check online, and you might be surprised. So many people sell their Instant Pots because they get frustrated with learning how to use them, and get overwhelmed and discouraged. Trust me, I was there too. Take the time to learn how to use it, and you'll soon learn that you might need two or three more.

## 9. I haven't used my machine because I'm afraid of it exploding on me!

Okay. I was there too. But you can't remove the lid if it's still under pressure. If you are able to remove it, you must be superstrong. There's a lot of pressure in that special little pot. Pay attention to the pin to make sure that your pot is depressurized, and you won't have anything to fear. Double-check that there's not pressure by making sure your vent on the lid is open and no more steam is coming out. Just know that lid has 10 or more UL Certified proven safety mechanisms to prevent most of the potential issues

## 10. I know that my machine is depressurized, but the pressure pin won't drop.

This happens sometimes. It means that something might have gotten stuck, and it's glued to the sides at the moment. Lightly tap the pin with the back of a butter knife. It should drop. If that doesn't work, try gently pressing on the pin to help it drop. Once you get your lid off, thoroughly clean the pressure pin area for any stuck ingredients.

## 11. Is there a difference between the Instant Pot and an electric pressure cooker?

Yes, there is! Yes, the Instant Pot is an electric pressure cooker, but it does so much more than that. You can make yogurt, proof bread, make beer, ferment vegetables and fruit, steam, sauté, brown meat, cook rice, use it as a slow cooker, and the list goes on. So it's not just an electric pressure cooker.

## 12. Does the Instant Pot really cook faster?

Yes and no. When it comes to cooking a succulent roast or pulled pork, it greatly reduces your cooking time and your meat doesn't dry out. However, there are certain foods it doesn't cook faster, like hard-boiled eggs, seafood, pasta, etc.

## 13. Can I use my Instant Pot as a fryer?

NO! Don't do this. Please. It doesn't meet any safety specifications for being able to fry anything in it.

## 14. What size instant Pot should I buy?

Great question! There are currently three different sizes that you can purchase: 3-quart, 6-quart, and 8-quart.
For 2 people or small side dishes, buy a 3-quart.
For family sizes 3–5, buy a 6-quart.
For family sizes 6 or more, buy an 8-quart.

## 15. Will my 3-quart Instant Pot have the same cooking time as my 8-quart one?

No. There will be different cooking times for any of these 3 sizes. When following a recipe, make sure you know what size Instant Pot that the recipe is using. All of my recipes used a 6-Quart Instant Pot.

## 16. My pressure-release knob came off. Now what do I do?

Rinse off and put it back in! It's meant to easily pull off to help with the cleaning process. Just be sure it's pushed back in.

## 15. If I want to double the recipe, do I have to double the cooking time?

No! You just have to add in a little bit more time. The time you add on really depends on the density of the meats and vegetables, and how much extra you're putting in there. Each case is different. If you're doubling up on the vegetables, then you shouldn't have to increase your cooking time at all. It would just take a little bit longer to bring it up to pressure. If you double up on the meat, then maybe add on a few extra minutes. It's very subjective, and you will become more comfortable as you continue using your Instant Pot.

## 16. My chicken turned out really dry; what's going on?

Well, the thing is that you're probably cooking your chicken in water. Water has no fat or flavor for the chicken. Try using a nice chicken broth, or use chicken breast on the bone with skin on. This will help ensure that your chicken isn't too tough.

The other thing is that you might have cooked the chicken too long in the Instant Pot.

Lastly, I've heard many chefs in restaurants give this hint: Don't cook frozen chicken. Can you do it in the Instant Pot? Of course you can! However, there is always a chance that your chicken might be a little dry.

## 17. Can I put my Instant Pot on the stove to cook?

Of course you can! Just *please* make sure that the stove isn't on! You'd be so surprised by how many people turn on one of the burners by accident, or place their machine on a hot top. It totally melts the bottom of the machine, and a lot of tears are shed.

However, I love using my machine on the stove because of the steam that comes out. The steam released won't damage any of my cabinets from the constant use. If you're done cooking on the counter, carefully move your IP over to the stove to release any pressure into the overhead vent. It works like a charm. You can always get one of the directional steam venters, but Instant Pot doesn't recommend anything that might block the flow of steam that comes out of the IP.

## 18. Wait. My machine doesn't have a Manual button on it. What now?

Don't worry. Different models have different terms. On certain Instant Pot models, it has the phrase Pressure Cook on it.

# Index